Bedtime Meditations for Children

Ann Margaret Walsh

Bedtime Meditations for Children
Copyright © 2022 Ann Margaret Walsh

Alderdawn Press

All rights reserved.

First Edition

ISBN: 978-1-7391826-0-1

Front Cover: www.123rf.com/blackspring

Kara Scrivener, Editor
www.emergingink.com

Without limiting the rights under copyright reserved above, no part of this publication may be reproduced, stored in or introduced into a retrieval system, or transmitted in any form or by any means (electronic, mechanical, photocopying, recording, or otherwise), without the prior written permission of the copyright owner.

To my three wee saplings:

Willow, Hazel, & Rowan

This is your little piece of Zen at bedtime.

Table of Contents

INTRODUCTION 1

MEDITATIONS FOR RELAXATION 6
MEDITATION 1: Rainbow Bright 7
MEDITATION 2: Movements to Sleep 10
MEDITATION 3: Snow Globe 12
MEDITATION 4: Piglet 15
MEDITATION 5: You Are an Octopus 18
MEDITATION 6: Boat Drifting on a Calm Sea 21
MEDITATION 7: Dinosaur Camp 23
MEDITATION 8: Desert Adventure 26
MEDITATION 9: The Ancient Forest 30
MEDITATION 10: Finding Your Own Space 33
MEDITATION 11: The Maze of Friendship 36

MEDITATIONS FOR UNLOCKING CREATIVITY 41
MEDITATION 12: Counting Sheep 43
MEDITATION 13: Swimming in the Coral Sea 45
MEDITATION 14: Captain of a Pirate Ship 48
MEDITATION 15: Giraffes in the Dublin Mountains 51
MEDITATION 16: The Secret Garden 54
MEDITATION 17: Exploring an Exotic Island 57
MEDITATION 18: A Walk through an Enchanted Forest 60
MEDITATION 19: Antarctic Adventure 63
MEDITATION 20: Your Very Own Adventure 66

Introduction

After discovering the power of meditation in my twenties, I have practised it ever since. I only wish I had been introduced to it earlier in life. I began creating meditational stories for my children to lower their anxiety levels, promote relaxation, and tap into positive thinking and creativity just before bedtime. My children enjoy the bonding time, and I love being able to guide them through the exercises.

What Is Guided Meditation?

Guided meditation helps someone create a mental image that focuses the mind in a particular direction. The goals of the meditations are to improve sleep, reduce stress and anxiety, build strong mental wellness, and unlock creativity.

How Does It Work?

Through guided meditation and the soothing sound of a trusted voice, children can slowly be introduced to mindfulness and taught how to harness the power of their imagination. Meditation cultivates a healthy lifestyle as it:

Promotes relaxation

Through gentle adventure, little ones are brought on a unique journey to a special space filled with tranquillity.

Improves sleep

It can sometimes be difficult to settle children in bed at night. Perhaps they are restless, anxious, or just uneasy about falling asleep on their own without someone by their side. Creating a happy and peaceful space at bedtime can make all the difference.

Guided meditation can reduce the likelihood of sleep disruption experienced during rapid cognitive development by helping your child drift off into a peaceful slumber. Sleep disruption may present itself in the form of nightmares, which can create an uneasy environment and make it difficult for children to settle back into a peaceful sleep once woken. Take the focus away from the cycle of frightening and disruptive thinking and shine the light upon positive and calming thoughts by creating a safe and soothing environment through guided meditation.

Reduces stress and anxiety

Stress and anxiety are real problems in today's world and affect children more and more from a young age. There can be any number of triggers but giving them the tools to deal with worrying or frightening thoughts can make all the difference.

Through practice, it is possible to learn how to stop the constant flow of thoughts and to work through any issues that are causing stress. Wouldn't it be wonderful to fall asleep without anxiety and wake up the next day well-rested, refreshed and full of energy?

Builds resilience

Building a strong sense of self-worth and confidence during childhood is paramount: to believe in the abilities you have been given; to acknowledge how special and unique you are; to be sure you are loved in this world by your friends and family. This all results in the development of a strong mental well-being that will stand the test of a lifetime. It is one of the best gifts a child can be given.

Unlocks creativity

Fast-paced living can make it difficult to find time for nurturing the creative process. By dedicating just ten or fifteen minutes a night to creative thinking, you will see the difference it makes.

Accessing the creative part of our mind helps us to be better problem solvers, which is an excellent life skill to possess. Children can mould and create a whole new world by utilising their imagination. Once they enter 'the flow,' they can unlock a myriad of desirable life skills.

How Do I Introduce Meditation to My Child?

The meditations in this book work best for children aged three to nine, but it all depends on the child. I have given a guide age for each meditation; you can alter the language to suit the ability of your child.

When introducing a new meditation, Take the time to answer any questions and explain the meanings of unfamiliar words so the child is comfortable with the language being used. It is best to stick with one meditation for a couple of weeks before moving on to a new one. This allows the child to relax into it and to be able to fully enjoy it through familiarity.

At the end of your usual bedtime routine, switch off the main light and leave the door ajar with some soft light filtering in from the hallway. A night light, salt lamp, or a dimmed desk lamp would also work well in the bedroom. A final story can then be read. Select a book with no pictures so the child doesn't feel as though they are missing out by lying down. This will allow their body to relax and their mind to slowly open and start to visualise the scenes and characters.

Before starting the meditation, ask the child to close their eyes. When speaking, use a low, soothing voice and allow long /

s to give the child time to imagine the different elements and to build the scene in their mind.

Siblings

Both the meditations for relaxation and the meditations for unlocking creativity can be shared by siblings in the same room. For the latter, each sibling can simply take a turn to answer the same question. Sometimes this can result in bigger and better ideas being gently bounced around the room. It can be a wonderful experience for siblings to share.

There are huge benefits to be gained and there is no time like the present to begin this journey – so let's get started!

Meditations for Relaxation

Meditations for Relaxation

The Benefits of Relaxation Meditations

These meditations not only help your child relax, but they introduce different adventures that can build a strong sense of self-worth and confidence. This sets the foundation for a deeper inner sense of calm and an innate ability to better manage emotions. Through gentle adventure, wrap your little one in a blanket of tranquillity, aiding a peaceful night's slumber.

Additional Relaxation Techniques

Additional techniques can be used to help your child relax.

A breathing exercise can be carried out at the beginning of the meditation. Focusing on breathing slowly in through the nose and out through the mouth can be effective in calming the nervous system and helping the body let go of any stress.

A gentle head, foot, or hand massage can improve relaxation and help settle the child for a peaceful night's sleep.

If your child is experiencing difficulty drifting off to sleep post-meditation, you can introduce ten minutes of their favourite calming music afterwards.

Positive Reinforcements

Positive reinforcements are included within the meditations with themes such as self-empowerment, embracing sibling love, nurturing strong family bonds, navigating friendships, accepting diversity, and letting go of worries or fears.

Meditation 1

Rainbow Bright

Guide Age: 3+
Themes: Contentment, safety, happiness
Concepts: Colours, summer, rainbows

This meditation creates a warm, happy, and calming atmosphere by introducing a tranquil green field illuminated by the vibrant colours of a rainbow. It's sure to promote a peaceful night's sleep that will recharge depleted energy levels. Positive messages of self-worth, contentment, and the joy in spreading happiness create an echo that can be heard and felt into the following day and beyond.

Close your eyes. And take a deep breath…
In through your nose…
And out through your mouth.
In through your nose…
And out through your mouth.…

Imagine you are walking in a field in the countryside…

There are green rolling hills far ahead of you,
Green fields all around you.
And up, up, up in the sky above,
There is a giant rainbow!

The colours are so bright.
You move as close as you can to the rainbow…
until you are standing directly underneath it.

You can see…
Red… orange… yellow… green… blue… indigo… and violet…

You lie down on the grass directly beneath the rainbow.
You can feel the colours shining their warmth upon you now.
You feel warm…
And cosy…
And safe.

Happiness starts to grow inside you. You can feel it start in your tummy and begin to spread throughout your body,
Reaching your face… and the top of your head.
Reaching your hands… and the tips of your fingers.
Reaching your feet… and the tips of your toes.
Your body feels calm and relaxed.

Notice your favourite rainbow colour in your mind now…
And watch as that colour begins to glow more brightly than the others.
It glows brighter and brighter…
Until finally it is the only colour you can see.
Focus on that colour now for a moment.

You can feel the energy of this colour shining upon you…
Giving you great comfort, strength, and hope.

Suddenly, you can feel how special you are…
How important you are…
How loved you are…
There is no one in this world like you.
Take a moment to appreciate who you are as a person.
You have many colours within your heart.
Shine your colours upon the world…

And be seen.
Share the happiness you feel inside with others…
Smile…
And the whole world will smile too…

Ever so slowly, your favourite colour starts to fade…
All the colours grow fainter and fainter…
Now, all that is left above you is a blue sky
And a bright yellow sun.

Your body is still resting on the soft warm grass…
You can feel the grass brush against your cheek…
Your body feels light…
And you begin to feel very sleepy…
One… two… three…
It is now time for sleep…
Goodnight and sleep tight!

Meditation 2

Movements to Sleep

Guide Age: 3+
Themes: Relaxation, sleepiness, beginner meditation
Concepts: Bedtime rest, body awareness

This meditation introduces children to mindfulness and promotes deep relaxation. It can be used as a standalone piece or be introduced at the end of any of the other relaxation meditations.

Close your eyes…
And take a deep breath…
In through your nose…
And out through your mouth.
In through your nose…
And out through your mouth…

Take a moment to feel your belly slowly rise and fall with each breath that you take…

Sleepiness is now beginning to travel up through your body…
Moving from your toes… to the soles of your feet… and on to the heels of your feet…
Moving up through your ankles… to your calves…
Up to your knees… then your thighs.
Your legs are feeling very sleepy now… very light and relaxed…

The sleepiness continues to travel up to your hips...
Reaching your back and your shoulders...
Flowing down into your arms...
Reaching your elbows... your wrists... and the palms of your hands...
Flowing down into your fingers... and then to your thumbs.
Your arms are feeling very sleepy now... very light and relaxed...

The sleepiness continues to travel up to your neck...
Reaching your head...
Then flowing to your cheeks... to your ears... and on to your temples...

Moving on to your forehead... to your nose... and your eyes...
Your eyelids are feeling very sleepy now...
As the sleepiness travels down your eyelashes... finally pulling your eyelids shut tight.
One... two... three...
It is now time for sleep...
Goodnight and sleep tight!

Meditation 3

Snow Globe

Guide Age: 3+
Themes: Uniqueness, individuality, fun
Concepts: Snow day, adventure, raucous play

This meditation creates a happy winter scene for the child where they get to experience playtime in the snow. The focus is on play, independence, and how good it can feel to build and create things by yourself. A positive reinforcement of how the child is unique and special is introduced, which can be effective through to the next day and beyond.

Close your eyes…
And take a deep breath…
In through your nose…
And out through your mouth.
In through your nose…
And out through your mouth…

Imagine you wake up one morning to hear that it is snowing…
You rush to look out through your bedroom window,
And you see the snow falling heavily outside.
You pull on your welly boots, your coat, and warm scarf and hat…
And race to the front door…

Excited, you run out into the snow.
The snow is so deep that your feet sink into it.
It feels like you are running in slow motion through a fluffy white cloud.
The snow falls heavy and fast…
You begin to twirl around and around, laughing as you twirl…
It feels as if you are in your very own giant snow globe!

You scoop a ball of snow up into your hands.
It feels soft and cool against your skin.
You make snowballs and throw them through the air.
You watch as they rise higher in the sky…
And then begin to fall towards the earth.
There is no sound when they hit the ground…
They just break into a million soft, tiny snowflakes.

You decide to build a snowman.
You roll a large ball for the body,
And a smaller ball for the head…
You find… one… two… three small rocks for the mouth…
And… one… two rocks for the eyes…
And you place a carrot in the centre of the head for the big nose.
One… two twigs for arms…
You have a tiara, a black hat, and a bandana in your hands.
You choose which one to place on the snowman's head…
And you finish it off with a colourful striped scarf where the head meets the body.
Your snowman is complete.

You run around the snowman…
Around and around and around until you feel dizzy.
You fall into the snow laughing and giggling.

When you look up, you are amazed to see your snowman
Dancing around in the snow… to your favourite song.
You giggle even more.
Watch your snowman for a moment as it dances around the garden.

It is time to make a snow angel…
You spread out your arms…
And your legs…
And move your arms as if you are flapping your wings.
Up and down… up and down… up and down…
Until you make imprints in the snow.

Standing up, you look down…
The imprint *does* look like an angel!
You watch as the snow wings begin to flutter…
Your snow angel rises up from the snow and flies into the sky.

You are amazed by what a fun day you have had.
It feels great to play on your own sometimes…
To build and create things,
To laugh to yourself,
To run and to jump.

The snow begins to fall again.
You watch as the snowflakes fall.
Each one is pretty and fluffy,
Each one is unique… just like you!
Think for a moment about how special you are in this world.

Snuggle into your bed now…
And imagine that the snowflakes are falling all around you…
Just like you are inside your very own snow globe.

Now… feel the soft pillow against your cheek.
You begin to feel very sleepy now… All cosy in your bed.

As you drift off, imagine what else you see in your snow globe…
One… two… three…
It is now time for sleep…
Goodnight and sleep tight!

Meditation 4

Piglet

Guide Age: 3+
Themes: Togetherness, family, safety
Concepts: Farm animals, pig family, adventure, exploration

This meditation creates a happy home environment by drawing parallels between a piglet's family life and the child's. The notion of "no place like home" is introduced, and the love that is unconditionally provided by a family is reinforced. This builds a sense of security for the child, reassuring them that they are a cherished part of the family unit. This love is carried with them into their daily lives.

Close your eyes…
And take a deep breath.
In through your nose…
And out through your mouth.
In through your nose…
And out through your mouth.

Imagine you are walking through a farmyard…

A friendly black and white sheepdog runs alongside you.
You can see a herd of goats in the opposite field, nibbling on clover.

Then you spot a flock of sheep beyond them, high up on a grassy bank…
They are grazing on the sweet grass and buttercups.
A black horse canters up to you as you pass by another field…
It pokes its head through the fence, wanting you to stroke it.
You rub its nose gently,
And then you pull a carrot out of your pocket.
The horse enjoys crunching on the juicy carrot.

This field is home to a herd of horses.
There are five black ones,
And chestnut brown ones,
And there is just one that is as white as snow.
You decide which one is your favourite…
Imagine what name you would give it.

Next to this field is a pen full of chickens…
They are pecking in the dirt and clucking.
You watch them as they have fun, squawking and flapping about.

A family of ducks waddles across the path in front of you…
The ducklings look so small and fluffy.
You stop to count them.

There is a strong smell of earth and fungus and old roots in the air now…
You realise that the smell is coming from the pig pen!
It is all muddy inside.
There's Mummy Pig…
And Daddy Pig…
And seven piglets.
The older piglets are all digging with their snouts in the mud,
Sniffing and chewing.
Mummy Pig and Daddy Pig are resting side by side in the little hut.
A baby piglet walks towards you.
You open the gate, and it jumps up into your arms.
You rub its little furry back

And tickle its tummy.
It snuggles into you.
You rub its little head slowly
Until finally it falls asleep.
You set the piglet down gently beside its family who is also resting…
You watch as the piglet snuggles among its siblings…
And Mummy and Daddy…
They all look so peaceful.

Like piglet, you feel safe and happy at home
With your family.
Your family loves you very much…
And you love them.
Home is a wonderful place,
Where you and your family are all together…
Happy and safe.

Snuggle into your bed now just like the piglet…
And feel the soft pillow against your cheek.
You begin to feel very sleepy now…
All cosy and warm in your bed…
One… two… three…
It is now time for sleep…
Goodnight and sleep tight!

Meditation 5

You Are an Octopus

Guide Age: 3+
Themes: Overcoming fear, exposure to new or strange, safety
Concepts: Ocean exploration, sea creatures

This meditation creates a unique chance to experience what it may be like for an octopus to swim and explore the seabed. This guided meditation constructs a connection to nature, which reinforces the message to care for and to love all creatures on our planet. A positive message--that we can overcome the fears we face in life--builds self-confidence and a sense of bravery.

Close your eyes…
And take a deep breath…
In through your nose…
And out through your mouth.
In through your nose…
And out through your mouth…

Imagine you are an octopus swimming in a warm, tropical ocean…

You can feel your eight tentacles moving,
Pulling you slowly and gently through the salty water.
You can feel your body move up…

And down…
As you swim.
You feel happy and free in the warm ocean.
You are on your way to your ocean home.
You move to the bottom of the ocean and,
Using your eight tentacles, you crawl across the rocks.

Take a moment to appreciate what a magnificent sea creature you are…
Did you know that you have no bones?
That you have blue blood?
And you have not one but *three* beating hearts?

Suddenly you can see flashes of colour begin to appear around you… What could it be?
Lots of tiny, colourful fish!
And they are swimming very close to you!
You wonder why there are so many.
Why do they all seem to be looking at you?

You feel a little overwhelmed and scared of all the fish…
So, you crawl into a tight space amidst the coral to hide.
You wish they would all disappear!
You decide to squirt ink out at them…
To try to make them go away.

Take a moment to think about why you might be so scared of those tiny fish? Especially since you are such a big and powerful creature…

Sometimes, we can be scared of things that are smaller than us…
Things that there is no need to fear…
Sometimes, if we take a deep breath and think for a moment, we realise there is no reason to be frightened at all…

You continue to swim home.

You are happy when you see your little rocky house between the stones.
Take a moment to imagine what colour your house is…
And what shape it is…
You wonder who else might live close by.

You feel safe and cosy now in your little rocky house…
Happy to watch the beautiful colourful fish swim past…

You begin to feel very sleepy now…
Watching the colourful fish swishing their tails
Has lulled you into a peaceful slumber…
One… two… three…
It is now time for sleep…
Goodnight and sleep tight!

Meditation 6

Boat Drifting on a Calm Sea

Guide Age: 3+
Themes: Uniqueness, love, friends and family
Concepts: Repetitive motions, soothing sensations, sea waves

This meditation creates a calming atmosphere by combining the motion of the waves and the stars shining down from the night sky. Positive messages of potential build optimism on waking and reinforces self-confidence in developing children.

Close your eyes…
And take a deep breath…
In through your nose…
And out through your mouth.
In through your nose…
And out through your mouth…

Imagine you are lying on the deck of a blue and white boat as it drifts quietly on the sea…

You can feel the coolness and the hardness of the wood against your back…
You can feel your body move up with the waves,
And down with the waves…

Up with the waves,
And down with the waves…

As you drift farther and farther off into the sea of sleep,
You look up at the night sky to find a trillion stars shining down upon you.
You are like one of those stars shining bright in this life…
You can do anything you want to do…
Be anything you want to be.
You are special… You are loved…
Your family loves you.
Your friends love you.
People who have yet to meet you will love you…

You feel your body move up with the waves,
And down with the waves…
Up with the waves,
And down with the waves…
As you drift farther and farther off into the sea of sleep…
One… two… three…
It is now time for sleep…
Goodnight and sleep tight!

Meditation 7

Dinosaur Camp

Guide Age: 4+
Themes: Adventure, exploration, problem solving
Concepts: Dinosaurs, colours, forests, hiking

This meditation is for the tiny adventurer as they are presented with an opportunity\i\ to travel back to the exciting time of the dinosaurs. The message within this guided meditation is that when problems present themselves, they can be more easily solved than we first thought. This gentle introduction to problem-solving can encourage children to be confident in finding solutions to challenges in their everyday lives.

Close your eyes…
And take a deep breath…
In through your nose…
And out through your mouth.
In through your nose…
And out through your mouth…

Imagine you are walking through a jungle…

As you walk, you bounce along the mossy, sponge-like carpet beneath your feet.
Trees with lots of leafy branches stand tall all around you.
Birds call out in song overhead.
You step through dense green foliage, many with colourful blooms…
Red… Yellow… Orange… Blue…
The smell of their perfume is marvellously sweet.

A small salamander lizard runs up the trunk of a tree…

As you step out from the canopy of the jungle,
A wind sweeps some of the colourful petals up, and they begin to swirl…making beautiful, colourful patterns in the sky.

Suddenly, you hear a loud shrieking noise!

At first you think it is just the sound of the wind, but as you look up into the sky…
You spot a red Pterodactyl flying overhead –
Wow!
It is flying with great speed, tearing through the sky,
Soaring fast, looping and diving.
After a few minutes, it seems to tire… and then it starts to glide effortlessly into the distance…
Until it finally disappears behind a snow-capped mountain.

You follow a path that leads you to a great rushing river…
But you realise you are not alone…
Nearby is giant Tyrannosaurus Rex!
You watch the great creature from the safety of the bushes as it moves away from you.
It looks very funny with a massive head and tiny arms…
And you are amazed by how big its feet are!
You take a moment to guess what size shoe it would take…
And imagine it in your favourite pair of shoes.
Wouldn't it look very funny?

You must cross to the other side of the river now
Because you must reach the Dinosaur Camp before you get too tired…
But there is a problem…
You cannot see a bridge!
How will you get across to the Dinosaur Camp?
You decide not to panic but to further explore
Then, you see it!
The solution to your problem…
It is a *glass* bridge! It was hidden in the sunlight!
You just had to take your time and look carefully to see it!

Sometimes, a problem can seem scary at first…
Sometimes, it feels like there is nothing you can do…
But sometimes,
If you take a deep breath
And think for a moment,
You will find the answer.
And sometimes, the answer is right in front of you.
Remember that you are clever,
You are bright,
And you will be able to find answers.
Just take a deep breath and take your time to think.

You walk across the glass bridge…
There is a large Diplodocus munching on grass…
And you see a baby Triceratops charging in play…
You imagine your favourite dinosaur and what it looks like.

At last, you see the Dinosaur Camp sign!
You crawl into your tent
And lie down in your sleeping bag.
You begin to feel very sleepy now…
The sounds of the jungle lull you to sleep…
One… two… three…
It is now time for sleep…
Goodnight and sleep tight!

Meditation 8

Desert Adventure

Guide Age: 4+
Themes: Siblinghood, sharing, family, adventure
Concepts: Desert, journey, desert wildlife, sand

This meditation creates a warm and adventurous atmosphere. The sun provides an energy that evokes positivity of mind, and the trek across the vast desert, first on foot and then by camel, inspires an adventurous spirit. In this guided meditation, relationships between siblings (insert brothers and/or sisters as appropriate to match the child's family) is celebrated. The positive messages of sibling love and friendship reinforce strong relationships during the day and introduce the idea that memories of the past are shared, future memories are to be cherished, and the present moment is to be celebrated together.

Close your eyes…
And take a deep breath…
In through your nose…
And out through your mouth.
In through your nose…
And out through your mouth…

Imagine you are trekking through a vast desert…

You can feel tiny grains of sand move

With a tickling sensation… between your toes…
As you walk slowly forward.
You are wearing a white flowing robe.
The airy linen fabric moves softly against your skin.
The hot sun shines in the sky high above…
The sun's rays shine with a great warmth upon your face.
Up ahead, there are sand dunes that stretch far into the distance.
Imagine what you might find in this desert…
What might be hidden behind the sand dunes?

You are not alone on this journey…
You can feel your *sister's* hand in yours.
There's nothing quite like the love of *sisters*.
Best friends that share a unique bond…
Share a home…
Share a family…
Share their time.

You are walking through this life together,
Sharing experiences that have passed
And experiences that are yet to come.
Remember that, together,
With double strength,
You can conquer anything.

Love each other…
Care for each other…
Be happy for each other…
And keep each other close…
And you will always have each other.
Sisters… best friends forever.

Suddenly, you see palm trees in front of you…
You walk through them to discover a beautiful oasis.
Colourful cactus flowers grow amidst the lush green.
Could there be water here? The source of all life…
Yes! You can see it!

A small pool of blue water right in the centre…
You dip your toes into the cool water,
And cupping your hands, bring some to your lips to drink.
You notice your reflection in the water
You smile, happy to see your own face.

You hear a noise, and you look up…
A camel strides slowly around the water's edge towards you and your *sister*.
It stops and lowers its long neck to take a drink from the pool.

When it is finished, it begins to walk once more…
You and your *sister* stand up and follow, as the camel moves into the cool, shaded area under the palm trees.
After a couple of minutes, the camel stops.
You notice it is carrying a large satchel made of woven fabric…
You open the bag to see what it contains…
You find…
An hourglass, fruit, a tent, and sleeping bags… in your favourite colours…

You build your camp for the night.
Together, you and your *sister* enjoy a fantastic feast of all your favourite fruit.
You hug each other as the sun drops from the desert sky
In a burst of vibrant oranges and pinks…
You watch as the colours slowly fade to a midnight blue…
And marvel at the brightness and brilliance of the stars shining down upon you.
Take a moment to think about how much you love your *sister*…
And about the things she does that makes you happy…

You climb into your sleeping bags…
Turning the hourglass, you invite sleep to follow…
You watch as the blue grains of sand leave the upper glass chamber…
And trickle…

Slowly…
Grain by grain… down through the narrow glass passage…
To the lower chamber.
Grain by grain… the grains of sand move and drop,
Move and drop,
Move and drop,
Until finally… there is no sand left.
You are swept away by the sands of time…
One… two… three…
It is now time for sleep…
Goodnight and sleep tight!

Meditation 9

The Ancient Forest

Guide Age: 4+
Themes: Family, unity, heritage, peace
Concepts: Trees, greenery, nature, brooks

    This meditation is set within the canopy of a great forest and explores the different elements of life. A serene atmosphere is created by connecting with the beauty of nature. The animals bring life; the trees foster strength; and the river encourages a gentle adventure into the unknown.

    A great comfort can be found in the idea that our ancestors and family members who have passed guide us through life. It can bring strength and create a wonderful feeling of safety and inner calm for the child, as well as sow the seeds of a deep-rooted respect for those who have come before and paved the way for them into this world.

Close your eyes…
And take a deep breath…
In through your nose…
And out through your mouth.
In through your nose…
And out through your mouth…

You find yourself walking in an ancient forest.

This forest is made up of many different types of trees.
Each of these trees has a story of its very own to tell,
The story of how they came to be…
And what has passed beneath their branches in their own lifetime.
You watch as the leaves of the trees… in varying shades of green and yellow…
Blow gently in the breeze.

Imagine what it would be like to be one of these trees,
What it would be like to have a trunk and leaves.
It might feel a bit different to have no legs or feet,
To have a trunk and be eternally in one spot.
Imagine what it would feel like for your leaves to blow in the gentle breeze…
It might make you feel calm.
Let your legs and arms become more relaxed now.

Did you know that you are part of a tree?
Your very own special *family* tree.
A long line of ancestors has come before you.
Without them, you would not be here.
They forged the way for you into this world,
And their love is always with you, wherever you go…
Protecting and guiding you.
Now, imagine their love as a white light.
It is glowing all around you.
Pull strength from this white light…
Whenever you need it.
Take a moment to be thankful for the family tree that you are part of.
Think of your mum and dad, your uncles, aunts, and cousins…
Grandparents and great-grandparents…
Even your great-great-great-grandparents who came long before you.
Now, continue strolling through the ancient forest…

Tiny twigs snap gently beneath your feet with each step you take.
Lush, green ferns brush your legs as you move forward.
A red squirrel scurries across your path to a nearby hazel tree.
You watch as it springs up and gracefully climbs the branches.

Birds sing in the branches high above,
A soft chirping that grows steadily into a harmonious melody that fills the entire forest.
The singing fills you with joy, and you smile…
Imagine what the birds might look like.?

You can hear water…
A babbling brook is flowing alongside you now.
The water rushes over rocks and stones,
Gurgling and whooshing as if part of a mighty race.
You follow the brook, and it leads you to the banks of a rushing river.

You sit down and rest your head against the trunk of a wonderful weeping willow tree.
The thin, hanging branches dance and sway gracefully in the breeze,
Dipping their slender leaves into the river,
Breaking the surface of water.

Catkins from the willow begin to fall slowly,
Tossing and tumbling through the breeze,
Eventually landing on the surface of the water… one by one.
You watch as the catkins slowly float away downstream…
Falling… then floating,
Falling… then floating,

You are feeling very sleepy now.
The current of the river sweeps your thoughts away…
One… two… three…
It is now time for sleep…
Goodnight and sleep tight!

Meditation 10

Finding Your Own Space

Guide Age: 6+
Themes: Wonder, awe, relevance, overcoming fears and worries
Concepts: Earth, space, stars, gravity

This meditation creates a safe, relaxing atmosphere in which to explore the parallels between space exploration and discovering the importance of a person's own space (or sense of self). This realisation of a happy personal space cultivates security and happiness, which reinforce a stronger sense of self.

Worries and fears can weigh on our spirit and body. In order to feel lighter and free, these worries and fears must be released. We can encourage children to visualise them as heavy weights falling away. This teaches young, developing minds that worries can be let go of and forgotten.

Close your eyes…
And take a deep breath…
In through your nose…
And out through your mouth.
In through your nose…
And out through your mouth…

Imagine you are floating in space, high up above the Earth…

Looking down, you can see our planet.
Notice how deep blue the oceans are
and how the land is a rich, lush green.
Think of all the people, plants, and animals that live on our planet.
There are so many different places where they all live.
Some live in the water, and some live on land.
What's one of your favourite places on the Earth?

Slowly, you feel your body grow lighter…
And you begin to drift father away from Earth…
Let your body become more relaxed now…
And watch as the planet Earth grows smaller and smaller beneath you.

You can see lots of other planets now.
There are many planets,
In many colours,
With many moons…

As you float farther into space,
Stars begin to appear all around you
twinkling in the surrounding darkness.

From the corner of your eye,
You notice that one of the stars is growing bigger and brighter.
The centre of the star is a magnificent yellow…
And then, it begins to burn a brilliant orange…
It is so vivid and captivating.
You cannot take your eyes away from it.
It is the most beautiful shade of orange you have ever seen.
It fills your full field of vision…
Take a moment to wish upon this star now.

Now that you've made your wish, the star shoots off into space,
And your eyes follow it…
You watch it as it grows smaller… and smaller… and smaller…
Until it finally disappears into the darkness.

Up close, things you worry about can seem large and overwhelming.
But just like a star fading into the darkness, your worries and fears
can grow small.
Picture a worry or fear in your mind,
Capture it there.
Now, imagine your worry or fear growing smaller and smaller,
Slowly hardening into one tiny moon rock in your pocket...
It is tiny, but it still feels too heavy to carry.
It weighs you down.
Toss the moon rock out of your pocket,
And watch as it tumbles,
Disappearing into the darkness of space beneath you.

You feel calmer and much more content now,
Floating free with only happy thoughts.
Picture one of those happy thoughts now
And enjoy the happy feeling it brings.

Take a deep breath...
You are floating... You can feel the space around you.
This is your very own space,
A calm and happy place
Where you can come to revitalise and recharge your energy.

Embrace your true self... You are wonderful...

You continue to drift lazily through space...
Your body feels oh so light...
As the gravitational pull becomes weaker and weaker...
You are weightless...
You are free...

As you drift off to sleep, imagine you are floating in space...
One... two... three...
It is now time for sleep...
Goodnight and sleep tight!

Meditation 11

The Maze of Friendship

Guide Age: 5+
Themes: Adventure, teamwork, making decisions, words of affirmation, self-assuredness
Concepts: Maze, problem-solving, pathways

This meditation explores the various natures of friendships: some friends are there from the beginning, some are lost along the way, and some are found later in life. Parallels are drawn between the paths of a maze and the paths taken through life. Being confident in decision making is paramount in reaching goals, but different decisions made in life can have a deep impact on friendships, either positively or negatively. True friends, however, who have taken different paths, will always reconnect with each other if they meet again.

We learn and experience new things through different friendships. As a result, we are moulded into better versions of ourselves. The positive messages of self and friendship build positivity on waking and reinforce a child's self-confidence.

Close your eyes…
And take a deep breath…
In through your nose…
And out through your mouth.

In through your nose…
And out through your mouth…

Imagine you are standing at the entrance of a hedge maze…
You notice that the hedges are tall and tower above you.
The leaves are deep green and dense.
There's no way you will be able to see over the hedges,
And it's impossible to see through them…
But you see this as a great challenge and are keen to enter.

Your friends arrive.
You feel happy to begin this adventure together.
You enter the maze.
Each time you choose a path,
Another path appears.
You must make a decision
To stay on the same path
Or to start on a new one.
Some of your friends pick different paths than you,
And that's okay.
You can make your own decision,
and they can make theirs.
Some decisions are tricky.
Some decisions are easy.
Sometimes, you choose a path that leads to a dead end,
But you just travel back along the path
And try again.

You reunite with some of your friends along the journey,
And don't see others for a long time.
But that's okay…
They are on their own adventures.
You also meet some new friends along the way …
It's always great to meet new friends.

You are a wonderful person,
And there are other wonderful people in this world.

Everyone is special to someone.
Know how special you are,
And that anyone is lucky to be your friend.

You have so much to give a friend.
You are kind.
You are clever.
You are funny.
You are exciting.
You are a great friend.
Offer your friendship to those who deserve it…
And you will receive great friendship from them in return.

You continue your journey
With a mixture of friends, old and new…
And you feel very grateful…
And happy
That you are all together.
You reach the centre of the maze
And celebrate with your friends.

You feel very sleepy now…
Dreaming of great friendships…

As you drift off to sleep, imagine you are having fun with your friends…
One… two… three…
It is now time for sleep…
Goodnight and sleep tight!

Meditations for Unlocking Creativity

Meditations for Unlocking Creativity

How Do These Meditations Work?

The following meditations provide the opportunity for your child to experience more control within the guided visualisations. They are taught how to unlock their own creativity, how to create a flow of ideas, and how to mould and shape these ideas. They will undergo a wonderful journey to an enchanting place, unique to them.

What Are the Benefits of Unlocking Creativity?

By nurturing their creativity at night for just five or ten minutes, you will see the benefits. Role-playing, make-believe games, and storytelling will become more fantastically novel and elaborate as children's concentration, positivity, and creative thinking improves.

Positive, creative thinkers are open-minded, more organised, and better at analysis. They can consider an issue in a new way and find alternate solutions, which make them excellent problem solvers. Creative problem solvers make the world a better place.

Creating a Different Focus

These meditations can be particularly useful to take focus away from a problem, worry, fear, or even a nightmare. The child's thoughts are refocused to be positive, calming, and happy—a sure way to drift into a contented night's slumber.

Improvise

Take the opportunity to improvise with these meditations. The suggested questions might produce answers that could prompt new and different queries. Follow a child's flow of thoughts and explore the inherent opportunities that present themselves. Use questions that require more information and further detail. This will help the new world to grow around the child.

Meditation Endings

Each meditation ends similarly with a counting exercise, which promotes a gentle push into a peaceful sleep. Vivid and beautiful dreams of adventure are sure to follow.

Meditation 12

Counting Sheep

Guide Age: 4+
Themes: Peace, imagination, counting
Concepts: Extensive fields, grass, sheep

This meditation draws upon the sleep exercise of counting sheep. The child creates their own picture of the field, setting up a calm and relaxing atmosphere, ideal for drifting off to sleep. The created scene allows for improvisation wherein a child can imagine what types of animals they see. Perhaps they want to count kangaroos jumping over the fence, dinosaurs, or even unicorns! You can tweak the meditation to suit the chosen animal.

Close your eyes…
and take a deep breath…
In through your nose…
And out through your mouth.
In through your nose…
And out through your mouth…

Imagine you are standing in a field…

What colour is the grass?
How long is the grass? Is it short?

Or is it up to your ankles? Your knees?
What are you wearing on your feet?

Look up at the sky. There are no clouds, just a very clear blue sky.

Is there anything close by in the field with you?
Are there flowers? Can you describe them?
Are there trees? Can you describe them?

Do you see the freshly painted gate? What colour is it?
Do you see the field on the other side of the gate?
Do you see the sheep in this field?
Do you see the hundreds of sheep in the other field?
Their fleeces are all soft and woolly…
Are they black sheep, grey sheep, white sheep, or a mixture of the three?

You sit on a patch of grass.
You can feel the grass gently tickling your legs as the breeze blows.
You feel incredibly happy.
Your body begins to relax.
The sheep want to cross into your field now…
Watch as they jump over the gate into your field.
Now count them in your head as they jump…
Tell me in the morning how many you were able to count.
Goodnight and sleep tight!

Meditation 13

Swimming in the Coral Sea

Guide Age: 4+
Themes: Exploration, speculation, adventure
Concepts: Mermaid/merman, underwater life, shipwreck

This meditation allows the child to create their own serene sea-world fantasy. Between mysterious sea creatures and abandoned shipwrecks, there is lots to explore. An appreciation for the seas and oceans and the creatures within them is nurtured. There is an option here to improvise and ask the child other questions about what else they observe in the sea around them. Tweak the meditation accordingly to follow the child's train of thought.

Close your eyes…
And take a deep breath…
In through your nose…
And out through your mouth.
In through your nose…
And out through your mouth…

Imagine you are swimming in the warm coral sea
When suddenly you begin to feel a tingling in your legs.
When you try to move them, you realise they have transformed into a tail!

This must be a magical sea, and you have turned into a mermaid/merman!

What colour is your tail?
What are you wearing?
What kind of hair do you have?

You venture underwater.
Can you see the tropical fish swimming past?
Are they small? Are they large? Are they colourful?

Look far into the sea ahead.
It is a brilliant turquoise, and rays of light filter through to the bottom.

You notice patches of coral.
It looks so colourful…
What colours can you see?

You swim into a nearby shipwreck.
What do you think happened to this boat?
Do you think there is any treasure? Can you find it?
What else can you see in this boat?

You swim out of the shipwreck.
There is a lot of seaweed on this side of the boat.
Do you see the octopus with the long tentacles crawling along the seabed?
Where do you think it is going?

You swim up to the surface.
Do you see the pod of dolphins jumping through the waves?
Will you follow them?
What other sea creatures can you see?
Wow! How amazing is that!
You begin to feel tired after all that swimming.
You take a deep breath and relax your body.

Your body drifts along on the waves,
The warm sea beneath your back.
It is time to search for pearls now,
So, you gently flip over
And swim to where the starfish decorate rocks.
As you come up onto the shore, you feel your tail begin to tingle and your legs return.
You are happy to be back to yourself again!

You climb over the rocks and begin searching the oyster shells for pearls.
Now count them one by one in your head as you find them…
And tell me in the morning how many you found.
Goodnight and sleep tight!

Meditation 14

Captain of a Pirate Ship

Guide Age: 4+
Themes: Adventure, leadership, exploration
Concepts: Pirates, ships, treasure

Adventure is at the heart of this meditation. Climb aboard a pirate ship on a voyage to find treasure. This meditation brings the child on a wonderful journey unique to them. There is an option here to improvise and ask the child other questions: what are the names of some of the crew members and what work do each of them do onboard the ship? What else can be seen through the golden spyglass? Ask questions to uncover details while following the child's train of thought.

Close your eyes…
And take a deep breath…
In through your nose…
And out through your mouth.
In through your nose…
And out through your mouth…

Imagine you are the feared captain of a mighty pirate ship…

A skull-and-crossbones flag flies high above your head on a mast.

What is the name of your ship?
Look down at your clothes.
What are you wearing?
A parrot flies through the sky and perches on your shoulder.
What colour is it?
What is your parrot's name?

Your crew is working hard to sail the ship.
Can you describe what your crew looks like?
What are they doing?

You set sail in search of treasure…
What kind of treasure is it?
(Gold? Jewels? Something else?)
You pull out your treasure map.
Can you see where X marks the spot of the buried treasure?
What else can you see on the map?

You take out your golden spyglass,
You look far out over the ocean.
It is a clear, blue day…
You can see the horizon where the ocean meets the sky.
Can you see the island appearing on the horizon?
Can you describe it?
Are there trees on the island? Flowers?
Do you think there is anyone else on the island? (If yes, who? Why are they there?)

You notice something in the sea up ahead.
Can you see all those jagged rocks?
Your ship would be much too wide to pass through them.
You must send the best swimmers in your crew to navigate through these rocks.
They will retrieve the treasure on the island and bring it back to the ship.

Can you see the crew lining up ready to walk the plank?

They jump up and down on the plank, ready to dive…
Now count them… one by one… in your head
As they jump off the plank into the ocean.
Tell me, in the morning, how many pirates you were able to count.
Goodnight and sleep tight!

Meditation 15

Giraffes in the Dublin Mountains

Guide Age: 4+
Themes: Family, self-love, different perspectives
Concepts: Mountains, cold, snowflakes

Differences are what make us unique and special. This meditation encourages the child to embrace anything that makes them different and to lovingly accept others who may be unalike. If they can truly love themselves, then they can love others. Diversity makes this world a wonderful place.

There are many options to improvise here and to ask the child other questions: how many other giraffes are with them? How do the giraffes look different from one another? How do they feel – happy, sad, angry, or excited? What are their different personality traits? Is there anything else high up in the mountain with them? What else can they see when they look down at the city? Tweak the meditation accordingly.

Close your eyes…
And take a deep breath…

In through your nose…
And out through your mouth.
In through your nose…
And out through your mouth…

Imagine you are a giraffe living with your family in the Dublin mountains…

Stretch your tall neck up as high as you can
And gaze down upon the city below.
It is evening.

Can you see the lights of the city?
What else about the city can you see?
Are there any people?
What are they doing?

Notice the different houses along one street.
Look in through the windows.
What can you see happening inside?

There are vehicles driving on the roads.
What kind of cars or trucks can you see?
Where do you think they are going?

If you were to visit the city as a giraffe under the cover of darkness,
Where would you go?
Why?

It is wintertime on the mountain.
So, it begins to snow…
Thousands and thousands of tiny snowflakes tumble from the sky.

Did you know that you are as unique as one of those falling snowflakes?
Everyone is different.
It is these differences that make each one of us special.

You are very special.
You are loved.
Stand tall, and you will be able to see things from all perspectives…
Raise your head and be seen.
You will make a great difference in this world,
Just embrace who you are.
Love yourself,
And love others.

Can you feel the cold snowflakes landing on your nose?
Stick out your tongue and catch the snowflakes…
What do they taste like when they land on your tongue?

Look up at the snowflakes…
And count them one by one in your head as they fall from the sky…
Tell me in the morning how many you were able to count.
Goodnight and sleep tight!

Meditation 16

The Secret Garden

Guide Age: 4+
Themes: Wonder, curiosity, relaxation
Concepts: Garden, herbs, flowers, butterflies

This meditation exposes the five senses to a secret garden. Facilitate a growing interest and love for nature by intertwining details from a previous day's gardening (planting flowers, trees, or herbs) or nature outing (butterfly/flower/tree identification). There is also an option here to improvise and ask the child other questions about what they see in the garden around them.

Close your eyes…
And take a deep breath…
In through your nose…
And out through your mouth.
In through your nose…
And out through your mouth…

Imagine you are standing in front of an enormous wooden gate…

On the ground in front of you is a golden key.
Use the key to open the gate.

Beyond the wooden gate is a secret garden.

There are tall flowers growing amidst tall grass.
What kind of flowers can you see?
A small path winds through the vegetation.
You follow it.
Can you hear the gentle hum of the buzzing honeybees flying close by?
You can see their small, round yellow-and-black bodies
as they hover over flowers in search of sweet nectar.
Take a moment to think about your favourite type of bug …
Why do you like that insect so much?

You spot a small pond with a fountain in the middle of it up ahead…
Even from a distance, you can hear the water spraying onto the surface of the pond.
Take a moment to listen to the water…
Can you feel the cool spray of the water landing on your skin?
Look into the pond…
What can you see?
Are there any fish? What kind?
What colour are they?

Lily pads float on the surface of the pond.
Can you see frogs? How many can you see altogether?
Watch as they hop from one lily pad to the next.
Take a moment to count them in your head.
How many frogs are there?

Look more closely at the pond's water. Is it clear… or is it cloudy?
Your reflection begins to appear in the water…
What are you wearing?
You leave the pond and explore the rest of the garden.

There are lots of trees growing.
What kind of trees can you see?

Which tree is your favourite? Why?
Nestled within the forest is a small, stone cottage with a herb garden out front.
What type of herbs do you see?
You decide to taste one, so you pick it...
What does it taste like?

Suddenly, the garden is filled with hundreds of butterflies!
You watch as they flutter their wings.
What colours are they?
Do you know any of the species' names?

You begin to feel sleepy...
So, you sit on a small garden bench...
You breathe in the sweet scent of the honeysuckle flowers beside you.
With each breath, you feel your body begin to relax...
You feel so happy surrounded by all of these beautiful butterflies.
Now, count each butterfly one by one as it flutters past...
And tell me in the morning how many butterflies you were able to count.
Goodnight and sleep tight!

Meditation 17

Exploring an Exotic Island

Guide Age: 5+
Themes: Exploration, travelling, discovery
Concepts: Hiking, exotic islands, fossils, new wildlife

This meditation allows the child to create a whole new island using their imagination. Geography, botany, zoology, and visual arts are all present in this adventure. There is an option here to improvise and ask the child other questions such as what might lie to the east or west of the island, letting them explore in detail the island and its environs.

Close your eyes…
And take a deep breath…
In through your nose…
And out through your mouth.
In through your nose…
And out through your mouth…

Imagine you are an explorer…

Your job is to find new places and add them to the map of the world.

Recently, you heard some tales of an exotic island.

You are ready for your adventure.
What are you wearing?
It is time to pack your backpack.
You place your notebook into it.
You will use this to record important findings.
What important survival supplies will you take with you on your adventure?

It is time to travel to the island now.
Are you travelling by helicopter or by boat?
Describe the journey to the island.

When you arrive, you decide to search the golden, sandy beach first.
You unclip the small metal detector from your bag,
extend the handle, and use it to sweep the beach.
What do you find?
(Some sort of treasure? Coins? Lumps of precious metal?
Or just bottle tops and scrap metal?)

Along the beach, you find a collection of rocks, some of which have interesting fossils in them.
What type of fossils are they?
(Ammonites? Dinosaur fossils?)
Or a completely new discovery?

Now you want to explore the rest of the island.
You look through your binoculars.
What is the land like on this island?
Are there any mountains? What about grasslands? A desert?

You set off on foot.
There is a lot of different vegetation.
Describe the plants you see.
Wow! You discover a new species of plant!
Describe the new species.

What will you name this new species?

You decide to head north.
There are animals up ahead.
What types of animals are they?
Something is moving, you see it from the corner of your eye…
Wow! You discover a new species of animal!
Describe the new species.
What will you name this new species?

You make your way back to the beach and sit on the golden sand.
Opening your notebook, you take your pencil in your hand and begin to draw.
You sketch all of your new discoveries one by one until your notepad is full.

You are feeling very tired now after all that exploring…
You lie on the warm sand.
Looking up at the blue sky, you can see white fluffy clouds begin to appear…
Count them one by one as they drift overhead…
Tell me in the morning how many clouds you managed to count.
Goodnight and sleep tight!

Meditation 18

A Walk through an Enchanted Forest

Guide Age: 5+
Themes: Celtic heritage, culturally-significant trees, self-assuredness
Concepts: Hazel/rowan/willow/oak trees, forest

This meditation draws on Celtic tree mythology to introduce messages of self-worth. A strong connection to nature is formed in the process and carried into the next waking day. There is an option here to improvise and ask the child other questions about their surroundings and/or to visit more Celtic trees: ash – a magical tree that spans between worlds, or hawthorn – a fairy tree.

Close your eyes…
And take a deep breath…
In through your nose…
And out through your mouth.
In through your nose…
And out through your mouth…

Imagine you are walking through an enchanted forest…

You look down to see that you are barefoot.
There is a carpet of soft leaves beneath your feet.
Can you describe what you see around you?

You are searching for our native trees.
These trees have been around for thousands of years,
And our Celtic ancestors believed each tree had a unique energy…

Your journey starts here…

First, you pass under the hazel tree.
The hazel tree is known as the tree of knowledge.
Believe in your own abilities.
Know how clever you truly are.
Listen to those with varied life experiences
And receive any advice gladly.
Your knowledge will grow
And so will your ability to make good decisions.
Walk on and know that you will gain great knowledge through your life.

Can you see any wildlife around you?
Can you describe what you see?

Your journey continues…

Next, you pass under the rowan tree…
The rowan tree is known as the tree of protection.
Know that you are safe and are loved by your family and friends…
In return, remember to show your love and support to them.
Continue through the forest, knowing that a great love surrounds and protects you.

Look up.
Can you see the red berries on the rowan tree?

What else do you see when you look up?

Your journey continues…

Next, you pass under the willow tree…
The willow tree is known as the wishing tree.
Picture what it is that you wish for,
See it in your mind's eye, noticing every detail of it.
And make your wish…
Know that if you work towards your dreams,
Anything is possible.

Can you see the stream beside the willow tree?
Describe it.
What can you see in the stream?

Your journey continues…

Farther into the forest, you pass under an oak tree…
The oak tree is known as the tree of strength.
Know that you have a great strength within you,
And you can tap into that strength whenever you need it.
You are powerful….
You are strong.
You can achieve anything in this life.

Now, reach up
And catch the oak leaves as they fall…
Tell me in the morning how many leaves you were able to catch.
Goodnight and sleep tight!

Meditation 19

Antarctic Adventure

Guide Age: 6+
Themes: Discovery, scientific research, adventure
Concepts: Artic, cold, ocean floor, penguins

This meditation allows the child to lead a scientific expedition into Antarctica. Walking in the shoes of a leader builds a strong sense of self-confidence. Geography, history, and zoology play a part in this unique adventure – Could it awaken a hidden interest?

There is an option here to improvise and ask the child other questions about their surroundings and/or about what else may be part of their research in Antarctica – animals, such as blue whales, albatrosses, leopard seals or krill, or landscape changes such as the shrinking of the ice sheets.

Close your eyes…
And take a deep breath…
In through your nose…
And out through your mouth.
In through your nose…
And out through your mouth…

Imagine you are the chief scientist onboard a boat
Sailing on an expedition to the Antarctic.

You need to dress very warmly where you are going.
Can you describe what you are wearing?

The sea is rich with wildlife…
Wow! Can you see the largest animal on Earth?
It's the blue whale!
Your team sends a robotic submarine underwater to find squid.
What colour is the submarine?
What shape is it?

You look at the computer screen to view the camera footage.
The camera on the submarine picked up some amazing images of a colossal squid!
You can see them now on the computer screen.
What do they look like?
Describe what else your underwater cameras may have captured.

Now, you must go in search of the emperor penguin.
You ask for the helicopters to be prepared.
The air is crisp, and the skies are blue – perfect for the journey.
You board the helicopter and await take off.
The blades begin to rotate faster and faster…
Up, up, up, and away.

You are travelling above the sea.
What does the air smell like? *(salty, minty, fresh…)*
Can you see the whales come up to breathe?
What types of whales do you see? *(orcas, blue…)*
Ice sheets float below.
Can you spot any fur seals on the ice?
What are they doing?

You feel so happy to be in the Antarctic exploring.
You remember some of the great explorers of the Antarctic…
Robert Falcon Scott and Sir Ernest Shackleton…
How do you think they felt exploring this region?
Do you think they were brave?

Do you think they missed home?
Your thoughts return once more to the emperor penguins…
What do you like most about penguins?
What would you like to learn about these animals?

At last, you reach the penguin colony.
You can see several fluffy, grey chicks cuddling into their parents.
For your research, you must count the penguins of the colony.
You have a counter in your hand…
Every time you see a penguin, you press the red button on the counter.
It makes a clicking sound.
You begin to count the penguins.
Click… click… click…
With each click, you grow sleepier and sleepier…
Tell me in the morning how many penguins you were able to count.
Goodnight and sleep tight!

Meditation 20

Your Very Own Adventure

Guide Age: 5+
Themes: Whatever you want it to be!
Concepts: Whatever you want it to be!

This meditation is created solely by the child.

Begin with a breathing exercise to promote relaxation:

> Close your eyes…
> And take a deep breath…
> In through your nose…
> And out through your mouth.
> In through your nose…
> And out through your mouth…

Ask some general questions to help the child visualise themselves in their own adventure. Some example questions to get you started might be:

Where are you?
What are you wearing?
What can you see?
What are you doing?

If your child needs help getting started, introduce a subject that interests them, such as:

Occupations	Astronauts	Chefs
	Pirates	Dancers
	Explorers	Farmers
	Doctors	Librarians
	Actors	Photographers
	Pilots	Veterinarians
	Zoo keepers	
	Teachers	
	Bakers	
	Writers	
	Firefighters	
The Supernatural and Fantastic	Superheroes	Fairies
	Unicorns	Werewolves
	Vampires	Witches/wizards
	Trolls	Mummies
	Dragons	Skeletons
	Ghosts	
	Elves	
	Gnomes	
	Centaurs	
Sports	Football	Tennis
	Swimming	Ice skating
	Dancing	Bowling
	Basketball	Martial arts
	Golf	
	Track/running	
	Volleyball	
Sciences	Space travel	Marine Biology
	Time travel	Palaeontology
	Botany	Astronomy
	Zoology	Geology
	History	Oceanography
	Geography	Meteorology
	Archaeology	Linguistics

As the child begins to build a creative world around themselves, specific questions can be asked to add detail. Avoid asking any leading questions as the aim is to allow the child to be in control.

The outcome is a wonderful adventure of their very own creation, a great way to exercise their imagination and open their mind to free-flowing thoughts.

Acknowledgements

There are a number of people who made this book possible. I wish to extend my sincere thanks for their support and encouragement.

My three saplings—Willow, Hazel, and Rowan—who continue to inspire me every day. I am so proud to see their interest and appreciation for the world and nature grow continuously. Without them, this book would not exist.

My amazing husband, Stephen, for his continued love and support.

My Editor Kara Scrivener at Emerging Ink Solutions for her enthusiasm and encouragement as she steered me through the entire process.

Finally, to Vanessa Fox O'Loughlin at Inkwell, and author Pam Lecky for their invaluable advice.

About the Book…

One night, my three-year-old daughter was having difficulty sleeping, so I decided to do a meditation with her, which was "A Boat Drifting on a Calm Sea". The meditation really calmed her and helped her to drift off into a peaceful night's sleep. Over the years that followed, I shared many more meditations with her and her siblings, and now there is rarely a night without one. They always ask for a meditation before sleep. We have a collection inspired by the subjects that they love, and I wanted the opportunity to share them with other families.

About the Author…

Ann Margaret Walsh is an author who lives in Dublin with her family. She studied both Science and Communications at University and has worked in many exciting roles within these fields. She has been on countless adventures around the world and always wants to travel and explore more places. Children's education and nature are particularly important to her and feature strongly in her books.

Printed in Great Britain
by Amazon